The Delaplaine 2021 Long Weekend Guide

Andrew Delaplaine

GET 3 FREE NOVELS
Like political thrillers?
See next page to download 3 FREE page-turning novels—no strings attached.

NO ONE HAS PAID A SINGLE PENNY OR GIVEN _ANYTHING_ TO BE INCLUDED IN THIS BOOK.

Senior Editors *Renee & Sophie Delaplaine*
Senior Writer **James Cubby**

Gramercy Park Press
New York London Paris
Copyright © by Gramercy Park Press - All rights reserved.

WANT 3 FREE THRILLERS?

Why, of course you do!
If you like these writers--
Vince Flynn, Brad Thor, Tom Clancy, James Patterson, David Baldacci, John Grisham, Brad Meltzer, Daniel Silva, Don DeLillo
If you like these TV series –
House of Cards, Scandal, West Wing, The Good Wife, Madam Secretary, Designated Survivor

> You'll love the **unputdownable** series about Jack Houston St. Clair, with political intrigue, romance, and loads of action and suspense.

Besides writing travel books, I've written political thrillers for many years that have delighted hundreds of thousands of readers. I want to introduce you to my work!
Send me an email and I'll send you a link where you can download the first 3 books in my bestselling series, absolutely FREE.
Mention **this book** when you email me.

andrewdelaplaine@mac.com

NEWPORT (R.I.)
The Delaplaine Long Weekend Guide

TABLE OF CONTENTS

Chapter 1 – WHY NEWPORT? – 4

Chapter 2 – WHERE TO STAY – 9
High on the Hog – Sensible Alternatives – Budget

Chapter 3 – WHERE TO EAT – 20
Extravagant – Middle Ground – Budget

Chapter 4 – NIGHTLIFE – 46

Chapter 5 – WHAT TO SEE & DO – 52

Chapter 6 – NEWPORT'S "COTTAGES" – 63

Chapter 7 – SHOPPING & SERVICES – 73

INDEX – 77

OTHER BOOKS BY THE SAME AUTHOR – 81

Chapter 1
WHY NEWPORT?

There are two wildly divergent sides to Newport that have always fascinated me.

On the one hand you have the quaint cobblestone streets lined with galleries, shops, cafés, stores filled with artisanally-crafted wares, tacky tourist traps, the port area where you're reminded that this was a place as connected to the sea as any weather-beaten town on the Maine Coast.

And then on the other hand, you have the "cottages," as the wealthy robber barons of the Gilded Age quaintly called their mega-mansions that make this town unique in all the world.

Back before the 1920s, you could walk up Fifth Avenue and see humongous townhouses owned by some the same families that built these summer "cottages" in Newport (most of which were occupied only for one or two months a year). Most of these houses were designed in the over-the-top ornate Beaux-Arts style favored at the time, everything, of course, copied from European styles America's wealthy sought to replicate with so much fervor in the eternal struggle to become "respectable."

In Manhattan, however, only a few of these houses remain. The Frick, for instance, at 70th Street and Fifth Avenue, is my personal favorite. Its interiors remain mostly as Henry Clay Frick left them except that they've been converted into galleries to display his vast art collection. Other New York houses, such as Andrew Carnegie's 64-room mansion built in 1902 on Fifth Avenue and 91st Street, have been repurposed as homes for nonprofit cultural institutions. In the Carnegie case, his house in now the Cooper-Hewitt Museum. (I've always found the house much more interesting than the exhibits mounted by Cooper-Hewitt sometimes daffy curators, but that's another story.)

    As I was saying, most of the houses lining Fifth Avenue were torn down only a decade or two after they were raised at such great expense. The real estate on Fifth Avenue just became so expensive that the families (after income taxes were introduced) decided to sell out rather than preserve these gorgeous houses an fine examples of period architecture. The big apartment blocks you see now on Fifth Avenue replaced those houses.

In Newport, however, the houses did not come down and a grand effort to preserve them was made. That's why they're here for you to marvel at today. And don't even think about coming to Newport if you don't make time for 2 or 3 of these wonderful houses.

Newport is home to any number of internationally recognized festivals and fairs, primary among them the Newport Folk Festival and the Newport Jazz Festival. Be sure to check out the schedules so you know what's going on during your Long Weekend visit.

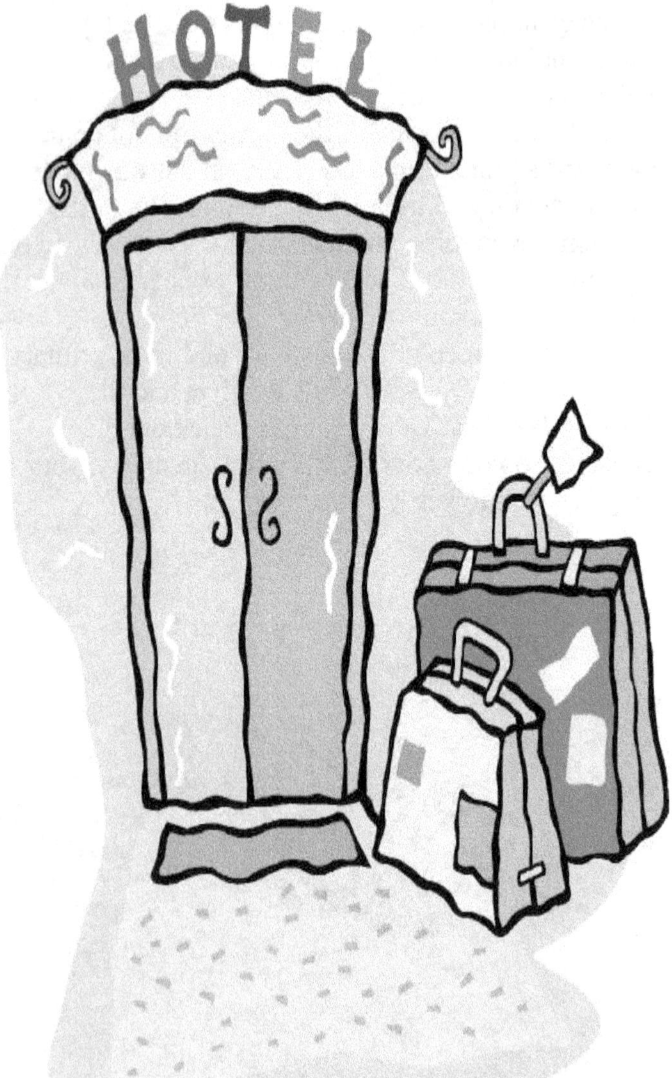
HOTEL

Chapter 2
WHERE TO STAY

DID YOU FIND AN INTERESTING PLACE?
If you discover a place you think I should check out on my next visit, drop me a line, will you? I'll mention your name if I end up listing it.
andrewdelaplaine@mac.com

ADMIRAL FITZROY INN
398 Thames St, Newport, 866-848-8780
www.admiralfitzroy.com
This premier getaway offers guests deluxe guestrooms in a European-style bed & breakfast. All rooms are decorated with antique sleigh beds and hand-stenciled armoires. Amenities include: free continental breakfast, private phone line, cable TV, small fridge, and free paring. Two-night minimum

required most weekends. Conveniently located near local restaurants and shopping.

THE ALMONDY INN
25 Pelham St, Newport, 401-848-7202
www.almondyinn.com
Conveniently located near Bannister's and Bowens Wharfs on Narragansett Bay, this restored 1890's Victorian inn features five elegant guestrooms and suites decorated with period antiques. Amenities include: Flat screen TV, DVD player, free Wi-Fi, signature bath amenities, free bottled water and daily maid service.

ARCHITECT'S INN
2 Sunnyside Pl, Newport, 401-845-2547
www.architectsinn.com
Constructed in 1873, this palatial guesthouse was originally the private home of George Champlin Mason, the famous Newport architect. Located on "Historic Hill", this Victorian mansion offers

beautifully appointed rooms, suites, and studios decorated in period furnishings. Amenities include: free breakfast, free Wi-Fi, free parking, and free breakfast. Massage therapist available. This inn also hosts Murder Mystery Weekends.

CASTLE HILL INN
590 Ocean Dr, Newport, 888-466-1355
www.castlehillinn.com
Located on 40-acre peninsula overlooking the mouth of Narragansett Bay, this restored 1875 mansion offers a variety of luxurious accommodations including a Swiss-style Chalet, Beach houses and cottages with a private beach. Amenities include: free breakfast, free Wi-Fi, and room service.

CLIFFSIDE INN
2 Seaview Ave, Newport, 401-847-1811
www.cliffsideinn.com
Nestled in the center of the historic district, this elegantly restored 1876 Victorian mansion inn offers beautifully designed guest rooms and suites. Conveniently located near local restaurants and shopping districts, this inn offers a beautiful getaway. Amenities include: whirlpool baths, spa showers, grand beds, LCD TVs, DVD players, iPod sound systems, a serene wrap-around porch, free gourmet breakfast, free Wi-Fi, and free parking.

FORTY 1° NORTH
351 Thames St, Newport, 401-846-8018
www.41north.com
This state-of-the-art hotel and marina is one of Newport's newest waterfront destinations boasting both restaurants and lounges. The resort hotel offers excellent accommodations with environmentally friendly amenities. All 28 guest rooms offer amenities like: gas fireplace, iPad, LED 40-inch flat-screen TV, free Wi-Fi, laptop compatible in-room safe, daily newspapers and desk-integrated media system. The resort features beautiful views of Newport Harbor and Thames Street. In-room spa services available. Pet friendly accommodations available. Valet parking.

GILDED
23 Brinley St, Newport, 401-619-7758
www.gildedhotel.com

NEIGHBORHOOD: Residential/Near Museum of Newport History

Located in a quiet residential neighborhood, this colorful eclectic 17-room boutique hotel (made up of 2 remodeled Victorian houses, one dating to 1850) offers guest rooms that look like they're from the Gilded Age, but have all the modern conveniences. (Only a few rooms have tubs, so be sure to ask for one if you want a tub.) A free breakfast is offered buffet-style every morning. Gilded is about a 15-minute walk to tourist spots on the water like the restaurant Black Pearl and others. Amenities: Complimentary Wi-Fi, iPod docks, smart TVs, iPads and complimentary breakfast. Hotel features: Guest lounge, secluded patio with croquet practice green, and billiards room. Conveniently located walking distance from the Museum of Newport History and 4 miles from the Ocean Drive Historic District. The owners here have a second property in Newport, the **Attwater**.

MARSHALL SLOCUM GUEST HOUSE
29 Kay St, Newport, 401-841-5120
www.marshallslocuminn.com

Repeatedly named by several publications as "Best Rhode Island Bed and Breakfast," this guesthouse continues to welcome satisfied returning guests. All six rooms are decorated with period antiques with amenities that include: Gilchrist and Soames toiletries, free Wi-Fi, free full morning breakfast, and free parking. Conveniently located just a short walk from downtown Newport and waterfront attractions.

NEWPORT BEACH HOTEL & SUITES
1 Wave Ave, Newport, 401-846-0310
www.newportbeachhotelandsuites.com
Formerly the Inn at Newport Beach, this hotel offers the largest and most luxurious guest rooms in Newport County. Amenities include: 37 inch LCD TV with HD DirecTV, HD DVD/CD player, MP3 player, iPod docking station, free Wi-Fi, and gourmet coffee and teas. Facilities include: indoor pool and whirlpool, fitness center with spa treatment room and rooftop hot tub and firepit. Located steps away from Easton's Beach and near recreation opportunities (skateboard park, aquarium and carousel). Private trainers and fitness instructors available. Free parking. On-site restaurant.

NEWPORT MARRIOTT
25 Americas Cup Ave, Newport, 401-849-1000
www.marriott.com/hotels/travel/pvdlw-newport-marriott

This Marriott offers first-class accommodations including perks like a full-service spa, an indoor pool, fitness center and on-site restaurant. This hotel offers 312 rooms and 7 suites on 7 floors. Amenities include: free Wi-Fi, daily newspaper delivery (on request), 32" HDTV, and a laptop safe. This is a smoke-free hotel. Conveniently located near beach facilities and sailing and golfing opportunities.

THAMES STREET GUEST HOUSE
15 Thames St (btw Poplar St and Bridge St), Newport, 401-846-8471
www.15thames.com
Originally an 1869 Italianate Victorian home, this Guest House offers luxurious accommodations. Amenities include: free Continental breakfast, Cable

TV, DVD, free Wi-Fi, an LED fireplace and air conditioning. Conveniently located near downtown Newport and waterfront/harbor areas. Two-night minimum stay on weekends.

HOTEL VIKING
One Bellevue Ave, Newport, 401-847-3300
www.hotelviking.com
This historic hotel offers a wonderful combination of old with modern comfort and amenities. Facility includes: Fitness Center, pool, spa, salon, Jacuzzi, and two on-site restaurants. Amenities include: free Wi-Fi, morning coffee in lobby and daily coffee in room, flat screen LCD TV, and gourmet honor baskets. Children's activities. Smoke free hotel.

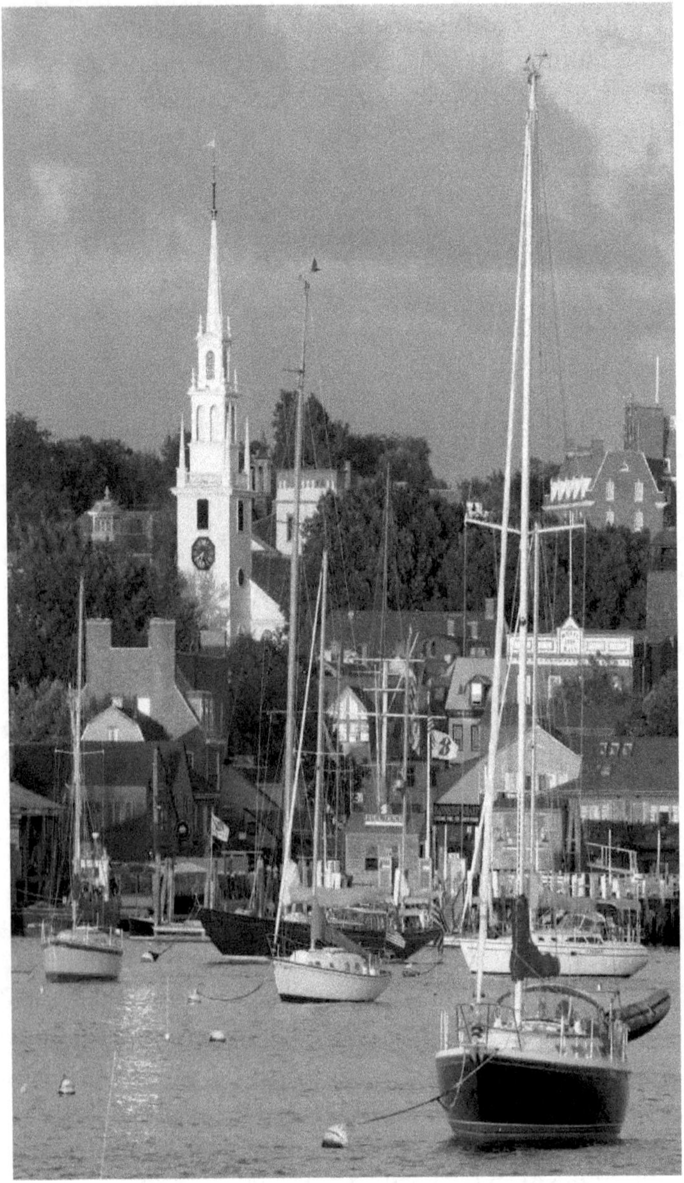

Chapter 3
WHERE TO EAT

DID YOU FIND AN INTERESTING PLACE?
If you discover a place you think I should check out on my next visit, drop me a line, will you? I'll mention your name if I end up listing it.
andrewdelaplaine@mac.com

22 BOWEN'S WINE BAR AND GRILL
22 Bowen's Wharf, Newport, 401-841-8884
www.22bowens.com

CUISINE: American (New)/Steakhouse
DRINKS: Full bar
SERVING: Dinner, Lunch & Dinner on Fri – Sun.
PRICE RANGE: $$$
Nautical-themed eatery serving fresh seafood and high-quality steaks. There's plenty of seating outside, but it's better to go upstairs and overlook the wharf area with all the boats—a better view, in my opinion. My Favorites: Rack of Lamb and Yellowfin Tuna, though it's hard to turn up your nose at the 18-oz bone-in Delmonico, and I didn't, because I rarely see that cut. (The streaks here are all Prime, by the way.) There's a great starter here, the Bucatini Carbonara, rich and satisfying, but a small enough portion so you don't ruin what comes after. Popular brunch destination on weekends. (Get the classic Wedge Salad, the bacon is great.)

BELLE'S CAFE
1 Washington St, Newport, 401-619-5964
www.newportshipyard.com/bellescafe
CUISINE: Cafe
DRINKS: No Booze
SERVING: Breakfast, Lunch
PRICE RANGE: $$
Boasting a reputation as the best place for breakfast in town, this café also offers a great lunch menu. Menu favorites include: Stuffed French Toast (breakfast) and Jamaican Jerk Chicken (lunch). Great daily specials. Guests get a great view of the Newport Bridge and can watch the yachts come in and out.

BENJAMIN'S RESTAURANT AND RAW BAR
254 Thames St, Newport, 401-846-8768
www.benjaminsrawbar.com
CUISINE: Seafood
DRINKS: Full bar
SERVING: Breakfast, Lunch & Dinner
PRICE RANGE: $$
Casual three-level eatery with a seafood focus. Raw bar. My Favorites: Lobster and Prime Rib. Daily happy hour specials.

BRICK ALLEY PUB
140 Thames St, Newport, 401 849-6334
www.brickalley.com
CUISINE: American
DRINKS: Full Bar
SERVING: Lunch, Dinner
PRICE RANGE: $$
Here you'll find a comfortable place to dine plus a great menu of "pub style" comfort food, steaks, pizza, pasta, and local seafood. The wine list includes over 250 vintages.
Menu My Favorites: Buffalo Chicken pizza and Lemony Chicken Piccata. The bar serves an impressive variety of creative cocktails like the Chocolate Mint Cookie, a sweet cocktail with a punch. Gluten-free menu available.

BUSKERS IRISH PUB
178 Thames St, Newport, 401-846-5856
www.buskerspub.com
CUISINE: Irish
DRINKS: Full Bar

SERVING: Breakfast, Brunch, Late night
PRICE RANGE: $$
This old world style pub is decorated with Irish antiques and features live music on weekends. No longer serving just "pub" food, this place now boasts to be Newport's only gastropub. Menu favorites include: Filet Mignon wrapped in Irish bacon and Goat Cheese & Prosciutto Shrimp.

CLARKE COOKE HOUSE
1 Bannisters Wharf, Newport, 401-849-2900
www.bannistersnewport.com
CUISINE: Seafood, Sushi Bar
DRINKS: Full Bar
SERVING: Lunch, Dinner
PRICE RANGE: $$$
Located in an 18th century building, the Clarke Cooke House offers several dining options. The Porch, an elegant dining room, The Candy Store, a more relaxed dining situation located at harbor level.

Intimate cocktails are available at The SkyBar. Menu favorites include: Summer Sushi. The wine list includes over 400 selections, including everything from regional wines to vintage Bordeaux.

CORNER CAFÉ
110 Broadway, Newport, 401-846-0606
www.cornercafenewport.com
CUISINE: Breakfast/Pizza
DRINKS: No Booze
SERVING: Breakfast & Lunch

PRICE RANGE: $$
Popular locals' breakfast café. My Favorites: Portuguese sweetbread French toast and Florentine Eggs Benedict. Tasty wood-grilled pizza. BYOB.

CRU CAFÉ
1 Casino Ter, Newport, 401-314-0500
www.crucafenewport.com
CUISINE: Café/Sandwiches
DRINKS: BYOB
SERVING: 8 a.m. – 5 p.m.

PRICE RANGE: $$
Small café with an outside patio. Order from the blackboards on the wall behind the counter. Menu includes breakfast and classic comfort food dishes, and the menu changes seasonally. My Favorites: Irish Burrito; a BLT that will knock your socks off, with 2 eggs, smoked bacon, avocado, on a Portuguese roll; and Poached eggs with avocado toast. BYOB. (There's a liquor store across the street called Vickers where you can get a bottle of whatever strikes your fancy & they'll serve it to you here.)

THE DECK
1 Waite's Wharf, Newport, 401-846-3600
www.waiteswharf.com
CUISINE: American/Seafood
DRINKS: Full Bar
SERVING: Lunch, Dinner
PRICE RANGE: $$$

This dockside venue offers fine dining, live entertainment, dancing and an outdoor lounge. Menu favorites include: Pan Seared Sea Scallops and Braised Lamb Shank. Great place for seafood lovers and a nightspot for the 20-30 year old crowd.

DIEGO'S MEXICAN RESTAURANT
11 Bowens Wharf, Newport, 401-619-2640
www.diegosnewport.com
CUISINE: Mexican
DRINKS: Full Bar
SERVING: Lunch, Dinner
PRICE RANGE: $$
This casual eatery offers Mexican cuisine with a modern twist. Menu favorites include: Crispy Pork Belly Tacos and Enchilada del Dia (stuffed enchiladas of the day). Try their creative cocktails like the Passion of Spice (El Buho Mezcal, fresh passion fruit puree, Habanero infused tequila, sour and pineapple juice). Gluten-free menu available.

THE DINING ROOM AT CASTLE HILL INN
590 Ocean Ave, Newport, 401-849-3800
www.castlehillinn.com
CUISINE: American (Traditional)
DRINKS: Full bar
SERVING: Dinner
PRICE RANGE: $$$
Located in the hotel, this beautiful upscale eatery offers several prix fixe menu choices. My Favorites: Yakitori Pork & Beef duo and Seared Yellowfin Tuna. Great views. Impressive wine list. Wine pairings. Very elegant eatery for a special occasion.

Sign outside Flo's

FLO'S CLAM SHACK
4 Wave Ave, Middletown, 401-847-8141
www.flosclamshacks.com
CUISINE: Seafood
DRINKS: Beer & Wine
SERVING: Lunch & Dinner
PRICE RANGE: $$
Right across the Easton Pond in Middleton is this great place located in an old two-level beach cottage

that survived the hurricane of 1938. Like me, you've seen a lot of "nautical-themed" restaurants when you travel, and you can tell not a lot of thought went into decorating these places. But Flo's is literally crammed with cast off seafaring items, the walls plastered with everything from oars to life vests to buoys to various signs. It's fun just to walk into the place. There have been several Flo's Clam shacks over the years, but they keep getting destroyed by the many hurricanes that have battered Newport. They always bounce back. The business has been around since the 1930s, and the New England seafood they offer is great. There's a big raw bar upstairs, which is where I like to hang out. My Favorites: White clam chowder and Fish & Chips. Fried Clams is their specialty. You never tasted better.

Outside Flo's (above)

FLUKE WINE BAR & KITCHEN
41 Bowen's Wharf, Newport, 401-849-7778
www.flukenewport.com
CUISINE: American
DRINKS: Full Bar
SERVING: Dinner
PRICE RANGE: $$
This casual two-level eatery located on the water offers a fresh creative seasonal menu. Menu favorites include: Roasted Eggplant Puree and Duck Empanaditas. The bar serves creative cocktails and a nice selection of wines.

FIFTH ELEMENT
111 Broadway, Newport, 401-619-2552
www.thefifthri.com
CUISINE: American
DRINKS: Full Bar
SERVING: Dinner

PRICE RANGE: $$
This combination bar and restaurant offers a great dining experience in a casual atmosphere. The cocktail and martini menu is pretty impressive and the food menu is just as creative. Menu favorites include: Spinach Balls and Lamb Kebob Salad.

FRANKLIN SPA
229 Spring St, Newport, 401-847-3540
No Website
CUISINE: American
DRINKS: No Booze
SERVING: Breakfast, Lunch
PRICE RANGE: $$ / **Cash only**
This down-to-earth diner is a breakfast favorite. Open since 1999, this place serves breakfast all day and great lunch selections. Menu favorites include:

Lobster omelette and Shared Eggs Benedict. Always busy. Cash only.

JO'S AMERICAN BISTRO
24 Memorial Blvd W, Newport, 401-847-5506
www.josamericanbistro.com
CUISINE: American (New)/Seafood
DRINKS: Full bar
SERVING: Dinner nightly, with Lunch added on weekends
PRICE RANGE: $$
Nice cozy little spot popular with locals serving American fare and seafood. My Favorites: Onion jam burger; Duck & Lobster quesadilla; and Lobster carbonara. Creative cocktails like Caramel apple martinis.

LUCIA ITALIAN RESTAURANT
186B Thames St, Newport, 401-846-4477
www.luciarestaurant.com
CUISINE: Italian
DRINKS: Beer & Wine
SERVING: Lunch & Dinner, Dinner only on Mon & Tues; Closed on Wednesdays
PRICE RANGE: $$
Cute little place in an old brick building with authentic Northern Italian cuisine offering classic dishes as well as vegetarian and Gluten-free options. You definitely want to focus on the pasta dishes here, because they're about the best you can get in Newport. My Favorites: Pappardelle alla Carbonara with Chicken; Manicotti ether with 4 cheeses or with their delicious homemade Bolognese ragu.

MALT
150 Broadway, Newport, 401-619-1667
No Website
CUISINE: American (New)
DRINKS: Full bar
SERVING: Lunch & Dinner
PRICE RANGE: $$
Cozy little Pub/tavern offering a menu of New American fare. My Menu picks: Fish & Chips and Pan Roasted Cod. Great burgers. Delicious desserts.

More than 30 beers on tap with an impressive selection of specialty cocktails.

MAMMA LUISA RESTAURANT
673 Thames St, Newport, 401-848-5257
www.mammaluisa.com
CUISINE: Italian
DRINKS: Beer & Wine
SERVING: Dinner; closed Wednesday
PRICE RANGE: $$
Longtime favorite serving classic Italian fare. Their Gnocchi can't be beat. Monday & Tuesday night specials. Nice selection of wines – mostly from the region.

MIDTOWN OYSTER BAR
345 Thames St, Newport, 401-619-4100
www.midtownoyster.com
CUISINE: American
DRINKS: Full Bar
SERVING: Lunch, Dinner
PRICE RANGE: $$
This is a top-notch seafood multi-level restaurant with the largest raw bar in Newport. Menu favorites include: Caramelized Sea Scallops and Oven Roasted Twin Lobster Tails. First floor has live music. Very busy.

MISSION
29 Marlborough St, Newport, 401-619-5560
www.missionnpt.com
CUISINE: Burgers/Falafels
DRINKS: Beer & Wine

SERVING: Lunch & Dinner
PRICE RANGE: $$
Simple no nonsense eatery named after Billy Goode's '20s speakeasy called The Mission. Tasty burgers and falafels. Homemade popsicles, crafted beer and wines.

MOORING SEAFOOD KITCHEN & BAR
1 Sayer's Wharf, Newport, 401-846-2260
www.mooringrestaurant.com
CUISINE: Seafood
DRINKS: Full Bar
SERVING: Breakfast, Lunch, Dinner
PRICE RANGE: $$$
This charming seafood eatery offers an amazing dining experience featuring indoor and outdoor dining. Their wine list features many of New England's best and includes more than 600 labels. Menu favorites include: Croissant Lobster Roll and

Portuguese Roasted Cod. Gluten-free menu available. Reservations recommended.

PERRO SALADO
19 Charles St, Newport, 401-619-4777
www.perrosalado.com
CUISINE: Mexican
DRINKS: Full Bar
SERVING: Dinner, Lunch on Sun
PRICE RANGE: $$
This place serves great creative traditional Mexican fare. The portions are large and you won't be disappointed. Menu favorites include: Mexican Scallops and Sticky Ribs. Great margaritas and sangria. Reservations recommended.

POUR JUDGEMENT
32 Broadway, Newport, 401-619-2115
www.pourjudgementnewport.com
CUISINE: American
DRINKS: Full Bar
SERVING: Lunch, Dinner
PRICE RANGE: $$
Popular restaurant among locals, this place offers a creative menu featuring soups, salads, sandwiches, seafood, and pastas. Nice selection of craft beers. Menu favorites include: Gouda Cheese Fries and Thai Shrimp Curry Nachos.

RED PARROT
348 Thames St, Newport, 401-847-3800
www.redparrotrestaurant.com
CUISINE: American
DRINKS: Full Bar
SERVING: Lunch, Dinner
PRICE RANGE: $$
One of the city's most popular restaurants, this eatery offers an eclectic 20-page menu prepared in two separate kitchens. Located in a historic building, there are three floors of dining and four bars. Menu favorites include: Blackened Mahi Mahi and Mandarin Coconut Chicken. Bar menu features assortment of creative cocktails and frozen drinks. Popular for large parties.

RESTAURANT BOUCHARD
505 Thames St, Newport, 401-846-0123

www.bouchardnewport.com
CUISINE: French
DRINKS: Full bar
SERVING: Dinner; closed Tuesday
PRICE RANGE: $$$
Classic French eatery complete with white table cloths and menu in French. My Favorites: Rack of Lamb and Duck breast. Nice wine list. Everything is good here.

SALVATION CAFÉ
140 Broadway, Newport, 401-847-2620
www.salvationcafe.com
CUISINE: Varied
DRINKS: Full bar
SERVING: Dinner
PRICE RANGE: $$
Trendy eatery with a tiki bar outside when the weather's good. The cuisine served here ranges from

Mongolian BBQ baby back ribs to Teriyaki Salmon to Cajun Jambalaya, so it's kind of all over the place. I've been here several times and can attest that everything is carefully prepared and very good. My Favorites: Lemon Herb Brick Chicken; the Short-rib burger. Creative cocktails. Happy hour specials.

SARDELLA'S ITALIAN RESTAURANT
30 Memorial Blvd W, Newport, 401-849-6312
www.sardellas.com
CUISINE: Italian/Pizza
DRINKS: Full bar
SERVING: Dinner
PRICE RANGE: $$
Casual eatery serving up hearty Italian fare. Fresh seafood and a nice variety of pasta dishes. My Favorites: Prosciutto Pizza and the Meatballs. Large restaurant with outdoor seating. Locals' favorite.

SCARPETTA
GURNEY'S RESORT

1 Goat Island, Newport, 401-849-2600
www.gurneysresorts.com/newport/dining/scarpetta
CUISINE: Italian
DRINKS: Full bar
SERVING: Dinner only 4 nights weekly; Closed Sun, Mon & Tues.
PRICE RANGE: $$$
Upscale slick, modern hotel eatery offering classic Italian dishes expertly prepared by the team at Scarpetta, which now has a half dozen locations around the country. Very fancy, very nice, but not as expensive as you might imagine (not at this location, anyway). My Favorites: Duck & Foie Gras Ravioli that's sinfully rich and delicious; Seared Diver Scallops that melt in your mouth and the Loin of Lamb in an herb crust that bursts with flavors. Creative cocktails. World-class wine list. Patio with a harbor view. There are a couple of other options here at the Gurney Resort, like the **Lounge and Firepit** where you can have a quiet cocktail, or the **Pineapple Club**, which is their outdoor bar overlooking the water. All very nice.

SPICED PEAR @ THE CHANLER
117 Memorial Blvd, Newport, 401-847-1300
www.thechanler.com/dining
CUISINE: Seafood
DRINKS: Full Bar
SERVING: Breakfast, Lunch, Dinner
PRICE RANGE: $$$
Located in the historic Chanler Hotel, this seafood eatery features fireside dining with a romantic terrace. The venue includes an open-air kitchen, grand

fireplace, and great ocean views. Known for its signature "New England Tasting menu," guests select from an ever-changing menu featuring local New England fare. Menu favorites include: Free Range Half Chicken and Wild Alaskan King Salmon. Impressive wine list. Live jazz on weekends.

THE WHARF PUB AND RESTAURANT
37 Bowen's Wharf, Newport, 401-619-5672
www.thewharfpubnewport.com
CUISINE: Argentinean
DRINKS: Full Bar
SERVING: Breakfast, Brunch, Late night
PRICE RANGE: $$
Their porch is a popular place to watch the action on Bannister's Wharf however dining inside the cozy dining room is best. The menu of pub food also includes meat, seafood, and pasta entrees. Menu favorites include: Roasted Turkey Meatloaf and BBQ Pork Shoulder Mac N Cheese. There's also a raw bar and a gluten-free menu. The bar offers 28 bottled beers and micro brews and a list of creative cocktails. Live music on Wednesday nights.

WHITE HORSE TAVERN
26 Marlborough St, 401-849-3600
www.whitehorsenewport.com
CUISINE: American
DRINKS: Full Bar
SERVING: Lunch, Dinner
PRICE RANGE: $$$
Built in 1652, this is the oldest bar in the nation. This historic venue offers fine dining in an elegant setting.

There are two bars and you must try a Darn and Stormy, the unofficial cocktail of Newport. The Tavern features a contemporary culinary experience with a menu that includes fresh local fish, clams, and lobster. Menu favorites include: Lobster Mac & Cheese and New England Style Crabcake.

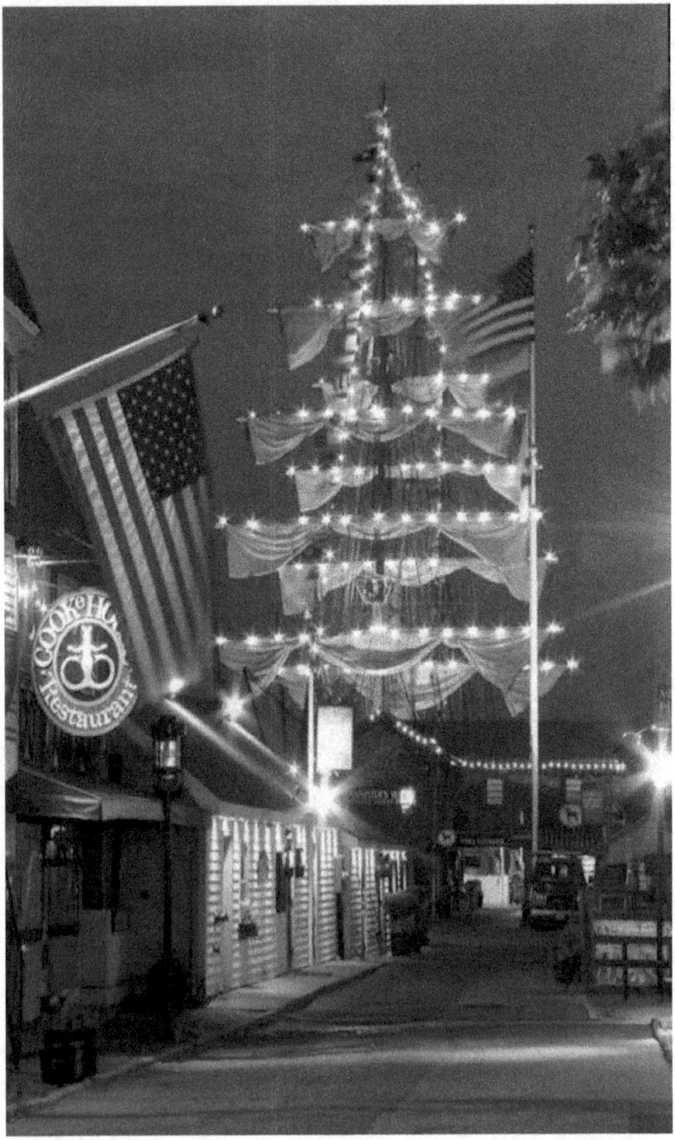
Restaurant

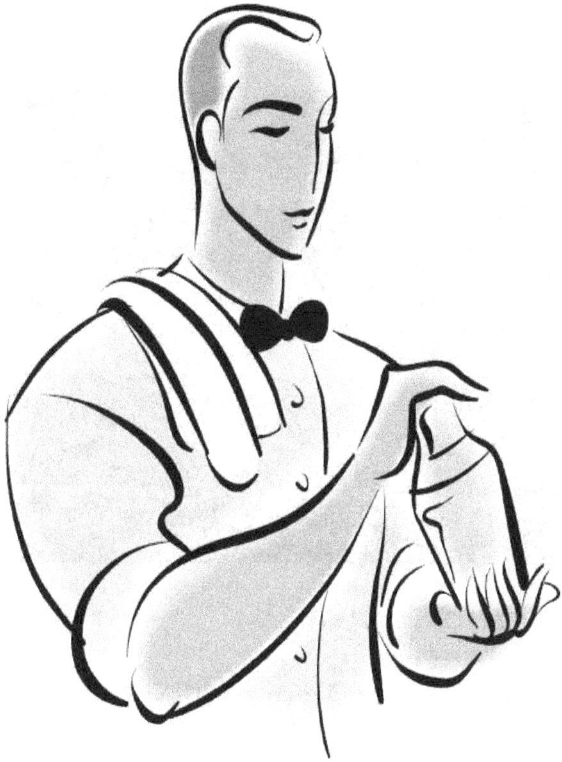

Chapter 4
NIGHTLIFE

DID YOU FIND AN INTERESTING PLACE?
If you discover a place you think I should check out on my next visit, drop me a line, will you? I'll mention your name if I end up listing it.
andrewdelaplaine@mac.com

BOOM BOOM ROOM
Clark Cook House
26 Bannister's Wharf, Newport, 401-849-2900
www.clarkecooke.com
Located in the basement of Clark Cook House restaurant, this nightspot offers music and dancing. This popular discotheque is very dark and attracts an eclectic crowd of all ages.

THE FASTNET PUB
1 Broadway, Newport, 401-845-9311
www.thefastnetpub.com
This popular local pub offers a variety of beers on tap, simple but strong cocktails, and a great place to catch the sports games on TV. Like your old-time pubs, this place has dartboards, a pool table, and a back patio for smoking. There's a simple menu of pub fare like fish and chips. Irish music night every Sunday.

NEWPORT BLUES CAFÉ
286 Thames St, Newport, 401-841-5510
www.newportblues.com/Newport_Blues_Cafe/Home.html
Housed in a historic brownstone built in 1892, this world-class, live music venue offers an impressive roster of local and national acts with a variety of music genres represented including classic rock, blues, progressive, indie rock and hip-hop.

O'BRIEN'S PUB
501 Thames St, Newport, 401-849-6623
www.theobrienspub.com
Located in the fifth ward district of Newport, this pub is a local's favorite for its bar scene but also offers a large menu for lunch and dinner. During summer season, the outdoor garden patio is quite popular and a great place to enjoy cocktails or dinner. The bar offers a variety of video games, pool tables and 5 TVs.

ONE PELHAM EAST
270 Thames St, Newport, 401-847-9460
www.thepelham.com
Open since 1975, this is Newport's oldest rock club. The place has booked its share of celebrity rock and reggae performers and has been a favorite hangout for the America's Cup sailing teams. Live bands and a dance floor. Open 7 nights a week.

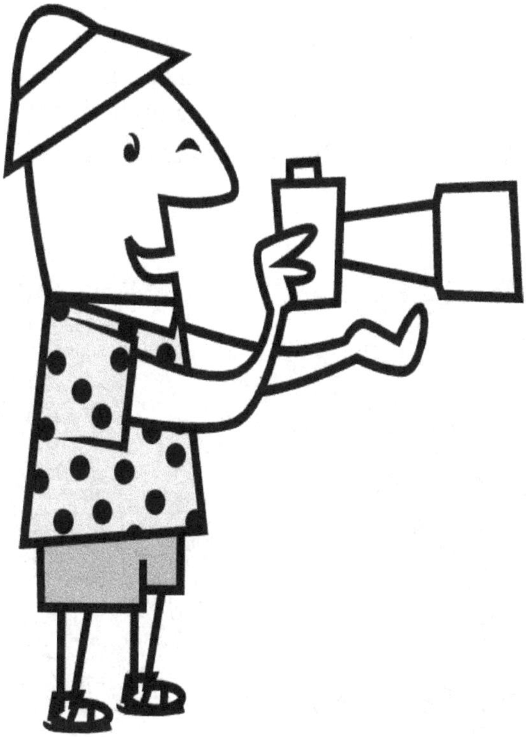

Chapter 5
WHAT TO SEE & DO

DID YOU FIND AN INTERESTING PLACE?
If you discover a place you think I should check out on my next visit, drop me a line, will you? I'll mention your name if I end up listing it.
andrewdelaplaine@mac.com

ADIRONDACK II
23 Bowens Wharf, Newport, 401-847-0000
www.sail-newport.com

Built in 1999 by Scarano Boat Building, this 80-foot boat is representative of a classic turn-of-the-century Pilot Schooner. A cruise aboard the Adirondack II is an experience as it passes Newport's stately bayside mansions, a 19th Century military fort and beautiful old lighthouses. This schooner can accommodate up to 60 passengers. Prices vary depending on the type of cruise. Available for corporate and private sailing charters, day sails and sunset cruises.

ANTIQUE YACHT COLLECTION
31 Bowens Wharf, Newport, 401-678-6740
www.antiqueyachtcollection.com
Private boat charter that offers a variety of VIP charter services. Private cruises for groups of six or less. What's really great are these beautiful old yachts exquisitely maintained.

AQUIDNECK GROWERS WEDNESDAY FARMERS MARKET
Memorial Blvd. & Chapel St., Newport, no phone
www.aquidneckgrowersmarket.org **WEBSITE DOWN AT PRESS TIME**
Open every Wednesday (June 4 – October 29, 2 – 6 p.m.) this weekly Farmers Market offers a great marketplace with more than 25 vendors selling both organic and conventionally-grown products including: fresh vegetables, cut flowers, herbs, berries, fruit, plants, eggs, breads, baked goods, meats, seafood, and cheeses. There's also live music.

ARBORETA TOURS
www.newportarboretumweek.org
Tour some of Newport's finest landscapes and tree collections at some of the best private Newport estates that open their grounds for tours.

BRETON POINT STATE PARK
Ocean Drive, Newport, 401-849-4562
www.riparks.com/Locations/LocationBrentonPoint.html
Occupying the former grounds of one of Newport's grandest estates, this park offers spectacular views as it's located at the point where Narragansett Bay meets the Atlantic Ocean. Visitors can enjoy the view, picnic, hike, and fish. Open year round. No fees.

BRICK MARKET HISTORIC DISTRICT
221 Goddard Row, Newport
www.brickmarketnewport.com
The Newport Historic District covers 250 acres in the center of that city with a selection of intact colonial buildings. The historic buildings include the city's oldest house and the former meeting place of the colonial and state legislatures. Set on Newport's waterfront, this is a favorite tourist attraction.

CLASSIC CRUISES OF NEWPORT
Bannister's Wharf, 401-847-0298
www.cruisenewport.com
Classic Cruises offers a great variety of water entertainment including sailing, powerboat tours and sunset cocktail harbor cruises. Cruises feature spectacular views of Newport Harbor and

Narragansett Bay. Choose from a 72' Schooner or a high-speed motor yacht. Modest fees depending on tour.

CLIFF WALK
www.cliffwalk.com
This scenic three and a half mile walkway borders the back lawn of The Breakers and several other beautiful Newport Mansions. This is one of the top attractions in Newport. The walk runs from the east end of Bailey's Beach to the west end of First Beach.

FORT ADAMS
90 Fort Adams Dr, Newport, 401-841-0707
www.fortadams.org

This State Park offers panoramic views of Newport Harbor and the East Passage of Narragansett Bay. Park activities include: saltwater bathing, fishing, boating, soccer, rugby, and picnicking. The park is known for its annual summer concerts. Permits needed to play rugby and soccer. Tours available.

INTERNATIONAL TENNIS HALL OF FAME AT THE NEWPORT CASINO
194 Bellevue Ave, Newport, 401-849-3990
www.tennisfame.com
Housed in the historic Newport Casino, this venue celebrates the history of tennis dating from the 12th Century to the present. The Hall of Fame has 18 galleries with over 20,000 square feet of interactive exhibits, videos, and tennis memorabilia. The collection contains over 16,000 objects. Open daily. Nominal admission fee.

JANE PICKENS THEATER
49 Touro St, Newport, 401-846-5252
www.janepickens.com
Located in Washington Square, this world-class art house cinema happens to be one of America's oldest theaters. The theater offers an impressive schedule of films, documentaries, and public events.

KRISTEN COATES ART & HOME
152 Bellevue Ave, Newport, 401-684-0211
www.kristencoates.net
Gallery & gift shop on Bowen's Wharf featuring art and objects for the well curated home including

contemporary art, collectibles and artisan made objects. Classes available.

MUSEUM OF NEWPORT HISTORY/NEWPORT HISTORICAL SOCIETY
127 Thames St, 401-841-8770
www.newporthistory.org
NEIGHBORHOOD: Historic district
ADMISSION: Free
The Society operates several historical facilities and supports and preserves, through documentation and exhibition, the history of Newport County. The museum, located in the 1762 Brick Market, offers an engaging introduction to Newport's rich history. Acting as an information center, this is also the departure point for guided walking tours. Exhibits include: James Franklin's printing press, photographs, furniture, colonial silver, paintings, and historical objects from the collections of the Newport Historical Society.

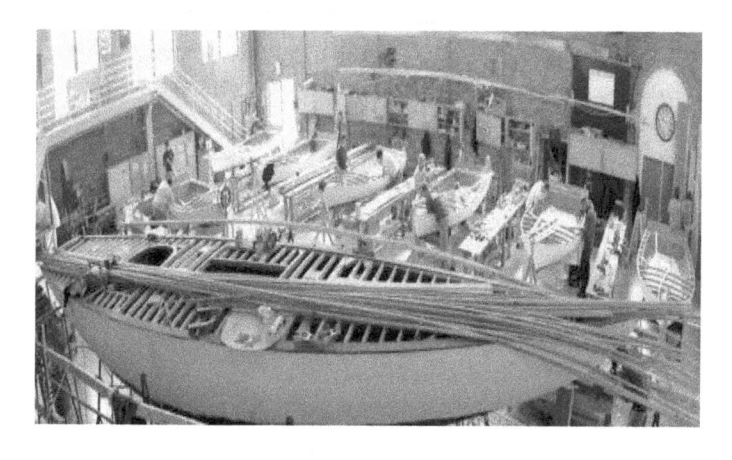

THE *M/V GANSETT*, GANSETT CRUISES
2 Bowens Wharf, Newport, 401-787-4438
www.gansettcruises.com
Cruises aboard the M/V Gansett offer a scenic tour of Newport and Jamestown. One and a half hour narrated harbor tours and sunset cruises available. Both cruises offer cocktails, beer and wine. The M/V Gansett is a well-appointed private yacht manned by well-informed guides. Price varies depending on cruise.

NATIONAL MUSEUM OF AMERICAN ILLUSTRATION
492 Bellevue Ave, Newport, 401-851-8949
www.americanillustration.org
Founded in 1998 by Judy and Laurence S. Cutler to house their art collection, this museum now exhibits art from all periods and styles. The museum building is an interpretation of an 18th century French chateau with three-acre grounds inspire by King Henry VIII's garden. The museum offers one of the greatest collections of American illustrations in perpetuity. Open year-round by advance reservation for group and VIP tours.

NAVAL WAR COLLEGE MUSEUM
686 Cushing Rd, Newport, 401-841-1310
https://www.usnwc.edu/museum
This museum's exhibitions celebrate the history of naval warfare and the naval heritage of Narragansett Bay. The collection museum offers exhibits pertaining to the genesis of the Navy in the region. Open daily. Reservations necessary made one

working day in advance. Non-U.S. Citizens require 14 days advance notice.

NEWPORT ART MUSEUM
76 Bellevue Ave, Newport, 401-848-8200
www.newportartmuseum.org
This museum celebrates Newport and Rhode Island's rich cultural heritage. The museum's permanent collection of over 2,300 works of American art focuses on 19th century to present day featuring artists like Howard Gardiner Cushing, Dale Chihuly, Richard Merking, James Baker, Rita Rogers and Sue McNally.
Nominal admission fee. Closed Mondays.

NEWPORT DISTILLING COMPANY/THOMAS TEW DISTILLERY
Coastal Extreme Brewing Company
293 J. T. Connell Rd, Newport, 401-849-5232
www.newportcraft.com
See firsthand how run is made and taste single barrel rum in the 3 stages of the aging process. The Visitors Center is open everyday (except Tuesdays) for tours and tastings. Visitors can view the distillery from the tour deck or enjoy one of the daily-guided tours (3 p.m.). Reservations not necessary. Nominal admission fee. Group private tours available.

NEWPORT GULLS BASEBALL TEAM
20 Americas Cup Ave, Newport, 401-845-6832
www.newportgulls.com
This is a wooden-bat, summer collegiate baseball team called the Newport Gulls. The team has won

several NECBL Championships. Check website for schedule.

NEWPORT HARBOR SHUTTLE
Newport Harbor Dr, Portsmouth, 401-847-9109
www.newportharborshuttle.com
Shuttle tour of the harbor starting at Perrotti Park by the Marriott. This 55-minute round trip tour makes six stops including Fort Adams. Tour guides are very informative. Minimal fee for the whole day allows you to hop off and get back on at no additional charge.

NEWPORT SHIPYARD
1 Washington St, Newport, 401-846-6000
www.newportshipyard.com
Full service boatyard and marina, ship store, restaurant and fitness center. You'll see some of the biggest superyachts on the East Coast docked here. It's fun to drop in at **Bella's Café** for breakfast or lunch.

NORMAN BIRD SANCTUARY
583 Third Beach Rd, Middletown, 401-846-2577
www.normanbirdsanctuary.org
Established in 1949 at the bequest of Mabel Norman Cerio, this 325-acre sanctuary offers diverse habitats to study birds. Guided bird walks available (every other Sunday beginning at 8 a.m.). Walks are free for members, a nominal fee is charged for non-members.

THE OCEAN DRIVE
www.oceandrivenewport.com
Ocean Drive offers ten miles of historic landmarks and breathtaking views of the Atlantic Ocean. Take RI-138 east or RI-114 south and follow the signs for RI-138A/Memorial Boulevard and turn right on Bellevue Drive heading south and the scenic drive begins.

REDWOOD LIBRARY AND ATHENAEUM
50 Bellevue Avenue, Newport, 401-847-0292
www.redwoodlibrary.org
NEIGHBORHOOD: Historic District
ADMISSION: Minimal Fee; guided tours Saturday at 10:30 a.m. – included with admission.
Founded in 1747, this is the oldest community library still in the original building in the United States. Besides beautiful books, the library exhibits paintings, busts, sculptures, and decorative arts. Two galleries feature revolving exhibitions.

ROUGH POINT
680 Bellevue Ave, Newport, 401-847-8344
www.newportrestoration.org
This is one of the Gilded Age mansions, formerly the Newport home of heiress Doris Duke; this beautiful oceanfront estate is now open as a museum. Still decorated as the infamous philanthropist and art collector left it, this mansion is filled with French furniture, European art, Chinese porcelains, and Turkish carpets. Tours last about 75 minutes. Nominal admission fee.

SAMUEL WHITEHORNE HOUSE MUSEUM
416 Thames St, Newport, 401-847-8344
www.newportrestoration.org
This Federal style mansion is open to the public as a historic house museum. The museum contains some of the best examples of Newport and Rhode Island furniture from the late 18th century including examples of craftsmen from the renowned Townsend and Goddard workshops. Open Thursday – Monday. Nominal admission fee, guided tours available.

TOURO SYNAGOGUE NATIONAL HISTORIC SITE
52 Spring St, Newport, 401-847-4794
www.tourosynagogue.org
Built in 1763, the Touro Synagogue is the oldest synagogue still standing in the United States and the only surviving synagogue in the U.S. dating back to the colonial era.
Nominal admission fee. Tours available. Closed on Saturdays.

WILLIAM VAREIKA FINE ARTS
212 Bellevue Ave, Newport, 401-849-6149
www.vareikafinearts.com
One of the largest and most respected galleries in the U.S. featuring 18th, 19th and early 20th century works of art, with items from Hudson Valley illuminist painters. Stained glass artist John La Farge is also featured here.

Chapter 6
NEWPORT'S "COTTAGES"

DID YOU FIND AN INTERESTING PLACE?
If you discover a place you think I should check out on my next visit, drop me a line, will you? I'll mention your name if I end up listing it.
andrewdelaplaine@mac.com

NEWPORT MANSIONS
The Preservation Society of Newport County
www.newportmansions.org
401-847-1000
This is a central website where you can explore some of the houses open to the public and buy tickets good to more than one tour.

If you only have time for 2 or 3 houses, tour the **Breakers**, the **Elms** and **Rough Point**. Those are my 3 favorites.

Also, if you have the time, I urge you to take the **Servants Life Tour** at the Elms. This tour focuses on the lives of the people who staffed these mansions. You'll hear the stories of the butler, Ernest Birch; his wife, cook Grace Rhodes; and one of the maids, Nellie Lynch Regoli. You have to climb up 82 stairs of the back staircase from the basement servant entrance to the third floor staff quarters, where you'll see exhibits and pictures of the people who lived and worked here. You even get to go out onto the roof where you'll get a stunning view of the estate and Newport Harbor beyond. The second part of the tour takes you back down the 82 steps where you'll see the basement kitchens, coal cellar, boiler room and laundry rooms.

Houses covered on the web site are:

THE BREAKERS
Cornelius Vanderbilt II, grandson to Commodore Vanderbilt, the family patriarch, built this house in 1893, and it's still the biggest of all the "cottages" in Newport.

MARBLE HOUSE
This is another Vanderbilt property, built by William K. Vanderbilt, to be exact.

THE ELMS
Built for Edward Berwind (a coal magnate from Philadelphia) and finished in 1901, this is a beautiful house modeled on the Chateau d'Asnieres on the outskirts of Paris. This is the house offering tours of the servants' quarters I mentioned above.

ROSECLIFF
Famed architect Stanford White (yes, the guy who got shot in the head at Madison Square Garden by his mistress's jilted lover) got the commission to built this house for Tessie Oelrichs, who inherited her money from her daddy, James Fair, who made it in the Nevada silver mines. (She was born in Virginia City, NV). The history of these Newport houses is also the history of the self-made billionaires of the Gilded Age, and there are dozens of colorful life stories involved. White used the Grand Trianon (a

garden getaway at Versailles where French kings relaxed) as his inspiration for this house.

CHATEAU-SUR-MER
This is one of the older houses, dating back to 1852, and was perhaps the grandest until the Vanderbilts started erecting houses in the 1890s. The house was built by William Wetmore, who made his money on the Yankee clippers that traded between the U.S. and China. Architect Richard Morris Hunt (the pre-eminent architect of the Gilded Age who went on to oversee construction of many houses in Newport and along Fifth Avenue) designed the house using influences from the French Second Empire.

KINGSCOTE
Dating back to 1839, Kingscote is the best example you're likely to find in the Gothic Revival style. Sure,

many towns have examples of this type of architecture, but they weren't built with the kind of money a Newport owner could throw at the project. It was built by a Southern planter, George Noble, but his family never returned to Newport after the Civil War broke out, and it passed into the hands of William King, another guy who made his fortune in the China trade. In the 1870s, the place was given a makeover by the distinguished firm of McKim, Mead & White (as in the aforementioned Stanford White). Some of Louis Comfort Tiffany's earliest work can be seen here in the translucent colored "bricks" he used.

Other houses covered are: **ISAAC BELL HOUSE, GREEN ANIMALS TOPIARY GARDEN, the HUNTER HOUSE** and **CHEPSTOWE**.

Other notable great houses in Newport not covered by the website above:

ASTOR BEECHWOOD MANSION
http://www.newport-discovery-
guide.com/beechwood-mansion.html
This was the Astor family's summer getaway place, now privately owned by a software billionaire and not open to the public.

BELCOURT CASTLE
http://www.belcourt.com/
Once owned by a Belmont, this house is in private hands once again.

OCHRE COURT
http://www.newport-discovery-guide.com/newport-mansions-ochre-court.html
This grand house (only the Vanderbilts' Breakers is bigger) is a little off the radar because it's owned by

the school, the Religious Sisters of Mercy. Descendants of the rich banker who built it in 1892 gave it to the church in 1947. You can go onto the grounds anytime you want and even have a look inside the house, where you'll be surprised at the grandness of the interior design.

ROUGH POINT
Newport Restoration Foundation
www.newportrestoration.org
This foundation was set up by Doris Duke, and it manages **Rough Point,** her oceanfront mansion here. This is definitely a worthy stop on your visit. Duke was the heiress, philanthropist and art collector. Enjoy her magnificent oceanfront estate, still decorated as she left it, where you will see French furniture, European art, Chinese porcelains, and Turkish carpets collected from exotic locations around the world. Located on Newport's exclusive Bellevue Avenue, Rough Point provides a sweeping

ocean view and expansive grounds designed by renowned landscape architect Frederick Law Olmsted, whose other little project in his life was designing Central Park in New York.

OCHRE COURT
(below)

Chapter 7
SHOPPING & SERVICES

DID YOU FIND AN INTERESTING PLACE?
If you discover a place you think I should check out on my next visit, drop me a line, will you? I'll mention your name if I end up listing it.
andrewdelaplaine@mac.com

BRAHMIN LEATHER WORKS
22 Bannister's Wharf, Newport, 401-849-5990
www.brahmin.com
This shop sells the handcrafted Brahmin handbag that is both elegant and long lasting. The brand is known worldwide. Here you'll find handbags and accessories.

COOKIE JAR
29 Bowen's Wharf, Newport, 401-846-5078
https://bowenswharf.com/directory/the-cookie-jar/
Since 1977, this little bakery has been selling sweets to locals and visitors. Here you'll find an assortment of fresh muffins, scones, cinnamon rolls, cookies, breakfast sandwiches, bagels, and banana bread. Of

course many come for the vast variety of cookies baked fresh daily.

THE MAGIC STUDIO
435 Thames St, Newport, 401-841-0735
This is Rhode Island's largest and only magic shop. Here you'll find top-notch magic sets, prank and gag gifts, juggling equipment and kites. A visit to this store is entertainment in itself.

NEWPORT SUNGLASS SHOP
BRICK MARKET PLACE
109 Swinburne Row, Newport, 401-846-6444
www.x-wear.com
This eyewear boutique is known as Newport's experts in sunglasses and eyewear. Hottest designer frames available like Smith Optics, Ray-Ban's, Oakley, and Maui Jim.

NEWPORT WINE CELLAR
11-13 Memorial Blvd E, Newport, 401-619-3966
www.newportwinecellar.com
Since 2008, this unique shop offers a great selection of high quality, small production wines from all wine producing regions. Weekly wine tastings and seminars are offered. Occasional offerings of craft beers.

PINK PINEAPPLE
380 Thames Rd, Newport, 401-849-8181
www.pinkpineappleshop.com
This boutique offers the Pink Pineapple cashmere collection designed by Stacie Hall. Here you'll find a beautiful selection of luxurious cashmere fashions as well as accessories, bracelets, and earrings.

PLEASANT SURPRISE
Brick Market Place
121 Swinburne Row, Newport, 401-846-1202
www.pleasant-surprise.com
Aptly named, this shop offers an eclectic mix of gifts, books, cards, toys, and home accessories. Most gift items have a nostalgic theme. Perfect place to buy a fun gift.
Shipping available.

TEN SPEED SPOKES
18 Elm St, Newport, 401-847-5609
www.tenspeedspokes.com
For more than 40 years this shop has been selling and servicing bicycles. This is a full-service bicycle shop that offers women's and men's clothing, shoes, sunglasses and accessories. Bicycle rentals available.

INDEX

2

22 BOWEN'S WINE BAR AND GRILL, 20

A

ADIRONDACK II, 52
ADMIRAL FITZROY INN, 9
ALMONDY INN, 10
ANTIQUE YACHT COLLECTION, 53
AQUIDNECK GROWERS WEDNESDAY FARMERS MARKET, 53
ARBORETA TOURS, 54
ARCHITECT'S INN, 10
ASTOR BEECHWOOD MANSION, 70
Attwater, 14

B

BELCOURT CASTLE, 70
Bella's Café, 60
BELLE'S CAFE, 21

BENJAMIN'S RESTAURANT AND RAW BAR, 22
BOOM BOOM ROOM, 46
BRAHMIN LEATHER WORKS, 73
BREAKERS, 65
BRETON POINT STATE PARK, 54
BRICK ALLEY PUB, 22
BRICK MARKET HISTORIC DISTRICT, 54
Brick Market Place, 75
BRICK MARKET PLACE, 74
BUSKERS IRISH PUB, 22

C

CASTLE HILL INN, 11
CHANLER, 41
CHATEAU-SUR-MER, 68
CHEPSTOWE, 69
Clark Cook House, 46
CLARKE COOKE HOUSE, 23
CLASSIC CRUISES, 54
CLIFF WALK, 55
CLIFFSIDE INN, 12
COOKIE JAR, 73
CORNER CAFÉ, 24
CRU CAFÉ, 25

D

DECK, 26
DIEGO'S MEXICAN RESTAURANT, 27
DINING ROOM AT CASTLE HILL INN, 27

E

ELMS, 67

F

FASTNET PUB, 47
FIFTH ELEMENT, 30
FLO'S CLAM SHACK, 28
FLUKE WINE BAR & KITCHEN, 30
FORT ADAMS, 55
FORTY 1° NORTH, 13
FRANKLIN SPA, 31

G

GILDED, 13
GREEN ANIMALS TOPIARY GARDEN, 69
GURNEY'S RESORT, 40

H

HOTEL VIKING, 17
HUNTER HOUSE, 69

I

INTERNATIONAL TENNIS HALL OF FAME, 56
ISAAC BELL HOUSE, 69

J

JANE PICKENS THEATER, 56
JO'S AMERICAN BISTRO, 32

K

KINGSCOTE, 68
KRISTEN COATES ART & HOME, 56

L

Lounge and Firepit, 41
LUCIA ITALIAN RESTAURANT, 33

M

M/V GANSETT, 58
MAGIC STUDIO, 74
MALT, 34
MAMMA LUISA, 35
MARBLE HOUSE, 66
MARSHALL SLOCUM GUEST HOUSE, 14
MIDTOWN OYSTER BAR, 35
MISSION, 35
MOORING SEAFOOD KITCHEN & BAR, 36
MUSEUM OF NEWPORT HISTORY, 57

N

NATIONAL MUSEUM OF AMERICAN ILLUSTRATION, 58
NAVAL WAR COLLEGE MUSEUM, 58
NEWPORT ART MUSEUM, 59
NEWPORT BEACH HOTEL, 15
NEWPORT BLUES CAFÉ, 48
NEWPORT CASINO, 56
NEWPORT DISTILLING COMPANY, 59
NEWPORT GULLS, 59
NEWPORT HARBOR SHUTTLE, 60
NEWPORT HISTORICAL SOCIETY, 57
NEWPORT MANSIONS, 64
NEWPORT MARRIOTT, 15
Newport Restoration Foundation, 71
NEWPORT SHIPYARD, 60
NEWPORT SUNGLASS SHOP, 74
NEWPORT WINE CELLAR, 74
NORMAN BIRD SANCTUARY, 60

O

O'BRIEN'S PUB, 49
OCEAN DRIVE, 61
OCHRE COURT, 70, 72
ONE PELHAM EAST, 50

P

PERRO SALADO, 37
Pineapple Club, 41
PINK PINEAPPLE, 75
PLEASANT SURPRISE, 75
POUR JUDGEMENT, 37
Preservation Society of Newport County, 64

R

RED PARROT, 38
REDWOOD LIBRARY AND ATHENAEUM, 61

RESTAURANT BOUCHARD, 38
ROSECLIFF, 67
Rough Point, 71
ROUGH POINT, 61, 71

S

SALVATION CAFÉ, 39
SAMUEL WHITEHORNE HOUSE, 62
SARDELLA'S, 40
SCARPETTA, 40
Servants Life Tour, 64
SPICED PEAR, 41

T

TEN SPEED SPOKES, 76
THAMES STREET GUEST HOUSE, 16
TOURO SYNAGOGUE, 62

W

WHARF PUB, 42
WHITE HORSE TAVERN, 42
WILLIAM VAREIKA FINE ARTS, 62

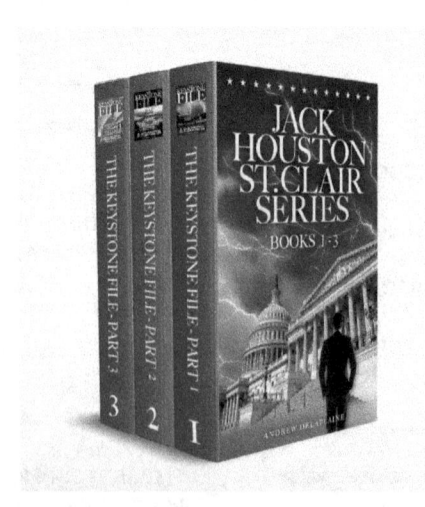

WANT 3 FREE THRILLERS?

Why, of course you do!

If you like these writers--

Vince Flynn, Brad Thor, Tom Clancy, James Patterson, David Baldacci, John Grisham, Brad Meltzer, Daniel Silva, Don DeLillo

If you like these TV series –
House of Cards, Scandal, West Wing, The Good Wife, Madam Secretary, Designated Survivor

> You'll love the **unputdownable** series about Jack Houston St. Clair, with political intrigue, romance, and loads of action and suspense.

Besides writing travel books, I've written political thrillers for many years that have delighted hundreds of thousands of readers. I want to introduce you to my work!

Send me an email and I'll send you a link where you can download the first 3 books in my bestselling series, absolutely FREE.

Mention **this book** when you email me.

andrewdelaplaine@mac.com

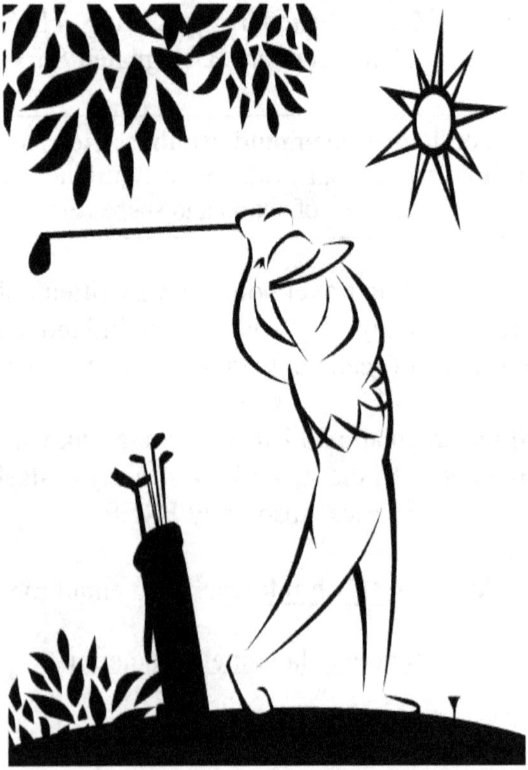

CPSIA information can be obtained
at www.ICGtesting.com
Printed in the USA
LVHW021313060521
686680LV00017B/1160